WOMEN SONGSTERS FROM EARLY CHINA

Book of Songs or *Shijing*

Translated

Richard Bertschinger
2024

Women Songsters from Early China
ISBN: 9798323872688
Copyright © 2024 (August) Richard Bertschinger
All rights reserved

Girl Feeding Fowl　Dazu Stone Carvings

Introduction

The whole of the Shijing comprises some 305 songs (or 'poems'): a compilation originally ascribed to Confucius (b.551 BCE). It is in four main parts: the *folksongs* ('airs of the states', *guofeng* 国风), the *lesser courtly songs, greater courtly songs* (*xiaoya, daya* 小雅, 大雅) and the *songs of the temple and altar* (*song* 颂).

In this translation I include only the first – 'airs of the states' or songs of the people - the greater number composed to be sung by women. Recording these 'airs' from the villages and surrounding country-side allowed the ruler to 'take the temperature' of the people; and, not surprisingly, these brief verses became 'the foundational corpus of early Chinese thought. As the most learned, memorized and most often quoted canonical tradition they became…the *sine quo non* of the educate elite during the Warring States (fifth century BCE – 221 BCE), the Golden Age of Chinese thought' (Hunter 2021).

What is most striking is that a greater number of then were obviously created and sung by women. I have extracted these for publication. A clear expression of the power of the feminine, of course, was very dear to the early Taoists.

ii

*The spirit of true nourishment never dies.
It is embodied in the deep power of the woman.
The pathway to this deep power
Lies at the root of all Heaven and earth.
Like a veil before your eyes and barely seen,
   its usage will never fail.* (Laozi 6)

*Yield and overcome, bend and be straight;
Have little and gain, have much and be confused.
Of old it was said: Yield and overcome.
Are these hollow words?
Why, once you conquer yourself,
Everything returns to you!* (Laozi 22)

*Homeward is the movement of the Tao,
Gentle, the power of her rule.* (Laozi 40)

*The weakest thing in the whole world can override
   the hardest thing in the universe.* (Laozi 43)

Michael Hunter (2021) in his *The Poetics of Early Chinese Thought* (see below) has spoken of 'returning home' as a dominant theme within the Shijing. Undoubtedly a love of homeland and country-life are dear to the hearts of the people who created these hundred-and-sixty songs. The same cannot be said of the rest of the work – which was more to do with empire-building and establishing a chronological legitimacy for the dominant Zhou rulers.

Primary among my sources have been, firstly, William Jennings, *The Shi King, The Old Poetry Classic of The Chinese,* Routledge and Sons 1891, which gave me the inspiration for this work (as I sat in my little mountain hut in the Bernese Oberland, though I had trouble with his Victorianisms!); Arthur Waley, *The Book of Songs*, Ed, Joseph R Allen, Grove Press 1996; Ezra Pound, *The Confucian Odes* (eschewing his extravagances), New Directions, New York 1959; the on-line James Legge (https://ctext.org/book-of-poetry/lessons-from-the-states); Steven Van Zoren, *Poetry and Personality: Reading, Exegesis, and Hermeneutics in Traditional China*, Stanford UP 1991; Michael Hunter, *The Poetics of Early Chinese Thought: How the Shijing shaped the Chinese Philosophical Tradition*, Columbia UP 2021; *The Shijing* (诗经) edited by Li Bo (礼伯), Beijing: China Federation of Literary and Art Circles Publishing House 2022; and the contemporary on-line analysis at https://shijing.5000yan.com/ which has been a great aid. Yet all failings, I fear, must be my own.

The numbering according to Mao, their first editor, is on the contents page as an aid to identification. In November 2024 I hope to publish the complete set of 160 Airs of the Old Chinese States.

Richard Bertschinger   Somerset 2024

Contents

	Mao	Page
Thickly grows the Cloth-grass	2	1
Pick and Pick the Mouse-ear	3	3
Pluck, Pluck the Thick Plantain	8	5
On the Banks of the River Ru	10	7
Gather in the Southernwood	13	9
Missing her Man	14	11
His Pious Bride	15	15
Walking in the Dew	17	17
Such Rolling Thunder	19	19
Left on the Tree	20	21
The Emperors Concubines	21	23
The Jiang has Arms	22	25
The Cedar Boat is Drifting	26	27
The Scorned Wife	27	31
O Sun, O Moon	29	33
Storm Wind	30	37
Gently Blows the Valley Wind	35	39
Those Spring Waters	39	44
Past The New Tower	43	47
Our Two Boys	44	49
Little She Understands Me	45	51
On the Wall a Thorn Bush	46	53
A Ruler's Wife	47	56
Quails Consort	49	59

Forth Must I Gallop	54	61
An 'Honest Fellow'	58	64
Thoughts of Home	59	69
Young Lad	60	71
Away at the Wars	62	73
There, That Lone Fox	63	75
My Old Man Marching Gone	66	77
Troubles in the Vale	69	79
The Wife's Affection	72	81
The Grand Carriage	73	83
Loitering Still	74	85
His Jet-black Robes	75	87
Master Zhong, I Pray you	76	89
I Followed Him	81	93
No-One Here	84	95
You Crazy, Crazy Boy	86	97
A Challenge	87	99
Misery Me	88	101
Beyond The Eastern Gate	89	103
Home Again	90	105
Left Just us Few	92	107
Creeping Plants Grow Wild	94	109
Spring Love-making	95	111
The Cock has Crowed	96	115
At the Gate He Awaits Me Now	98	117
Surely Not Him	108	119
What Might Tonight Bring	118	121
All Alone	124	123

My Thoughts are all with My Man	128	125
Where Reed and Rush	129	128
My Worried Heart	132	131
What a Night!	140	133
At the Margin of the Moor	145	135
Are You Still Loitering	146	137
The Fragility of Life	150	139

Thickly grows the Cloth-grass

葛之覃兮，施于中谷，维叶萋萋。
黄鸟于飞，集于灌木，其鸣喈喈。
葛之覃兮，施于中谷，维叶莫莫。
是刈是濩，为絺为绤，服之无斁。
言告师氏，言告言归！薄污我私，薄浣我衣。
害浣害否？归宁父母。

Gé zhī tán xī, shī yú zhōnggǔ, wéi yè qī qī.
Huáng niǎo yú fēi, jí yú guànmù, qí míng jiē jiē.
Gé zhī tán xī, shī yú zhōnggǔ, wéi yè mò mò.
Shì yì shì huò, wèi chī wèi xì, fú zhī wú yì.
Yán gào shī shì, yán gào yán guī!
Báo wū wǒ sī, báo huàn wǒ yī.
Hài huàn hài fǒu? Guīníng fùmǔ.

THICKLY GROWS the Cloth-grass,
Way down in the Valley,
Its Leaves so densely bound.
Look! the golden Orioles in flight,
Now gathering in the Bushes,
Their Cries so freely sound!

Thickly grows the Cloth-grass,
Way down in the Valley.
Its Leaves so close and lush.
I'll cut and steam them
Thus to make a fine Cloth,
Plain, but never to weary of.

I must let my Mistress know,
That soon I'm returning Home!
Soap and wash my Clothing,
Wash - then rinse my Dress,
Now which one will I wear?
To my Parents, soon I'm going!

The duties and anticipation of a well-born woman before her marriage. As she is in service she has to ask her mistress if she can leave.

Pick and Pick the Mouse-ear

采采卷耳，不盈顷筐。嗟我怀人，寘彼周行。
陟彼崔嵬，我马虺隤。我姑酌彼金罍，维以不永怀。
陟彼高冈，我马玄黄。我姑酌彼兕觥，维以不永伤。
陟彼砠矣，我马瘏矣，我仆痡矣，云何吁矣。

Cǎi cǎi juǎn ěr, bù yíng qǐng kuāng.
Jiē wǒ huái rén, zhì bǐ zhōu xíng.
Zhì bǐ cuīwéi, wǒ mǎ huī tuí.
Wǒ gū zhuó bǐ jīn léi, wéi yǐ bù yǒng huái.
Zhì bǐ gāo gāng, wǒ mǎ xuánhuáng.
Wǒ gū zhuó bǐ sì gōng, wéi yǐ bù yǒng shāng.
Zhì bǐ jū yǐ, wǒ mǎ tú yǐ,
Wǒ pū fū yǐ, yún hé xū yǐ.

'I MUST PICK AND PICK the Mouse-ear,
But I never get a Basket load!
My Heart is with my Husband.
I fling it on down the Road!'

'I was climbing the rugged Trail,
My Ponies too tired to go on.
I stopped to pour a Cup the Flask,
Not to think on Her too long.'

'I'm climbing 'long the steep Ridge,
With the Ponies, the Black and Bay.
Now take a Drink from my Horn-mug,
Hoping some Sadness it might allay.'

'Now I'm crossing the loose Shale,
But the Ponies are nearly spent!
The Foot Servants are exhausted,
Now is not the Time to repent!'

The first stanza shows the woman missing her man. The rest of the song is her husband speaking.

Pluck, Pluck the Thick Plantain

采采芣苢，薄言采之。采采芣苢，薄言有之。
采采芣苢，薄言掇之。采采芣苢，薄言捋之。
采采芣苢，薄言袺之。采采芣苢，薄言襭之。

Căi căi fú yĭ, báo yán căi zhī.
Căi căi fú yĭ, báo yán yŏu zhī.
Căi căi fú yĭ, báo yán duō zhī.
Căi căi fú yĭ, báo yán lǚ zhī.
Căi căi fú yĭ, báo yán jié zhī.
Căi căi fú yĭ, báo yán xié zhī.

PLUCK, PLUCK the thick Plantain,
I pluck, pluck, to gather it in.
Pluck, pluck the thick Plantain …
Here! now We have it!

Pluck, pluck the thick Plantain,
This is the way to clip it!
Pluck, pluck the thick Plantain …
This is the Way to strip it!

I pluck, pluck the thick Plantain,
Now gathered in our Skirts.
Pluck, pluck the thick Plantain …
Now bundled round my Waist.

A song showing the repetitive task of picking, shouted or chanted while working in the fields. In the West we had our popular 'sea shanties'. The scene comes alive with their singing!

On the Banks of the River Ru

遵彼汝坟，伐其条枚。未见君子，惄如调饥。
遵彼汝坟，伐其条肄。既见君子，不我遐弃。
鲂鱼赪尾，王室如毁。虽则如毁，父母孔迩。

Zūn bǐ rǔ fén, fá qí tiáo méi. Wèi jiàn jūnzǐ, nì rú diào jī.
Zūn bǐ rǔ fén, fá qí tiáo yì. Jì jiàn jūnzǐ, bù wǒ xiá qì.
Fáng yú chēng wěi, wángshì rú huǐ.
Suīzé rú huǐ, fùmǔ kǒng ěr.

ON THE BANKS of the River Ru I passed,
Gathering Firewood from the Trees.
I have not seen him in such a long time,
But if I cannot eat, I'll surely freeze!

Along the banks of the Ru I passed
To cut the Shoots that sprout anew.
I have just heard from my Man....
Do not reject Me as you can do!

Poor Bream! your Tail all flaming red!
Our Royal House ablaze I fear!
But whatever the Blaze -
The Family's Heart is near!

    The wife misses her husband and their reunion reignites her faith in the family. This is a very puzzling rhyme; the 'flaming red' tail is probably bleeding - an ill omen. Perhaps the 'flame' indicates feminine passion. Something not properly talked about in old China. The wife dutifully keeps the home going (firewood) – then reveals her worries about abandonment. The shoots 'sprouting anew' suggest a whole season passed.

Gather in the Southernwood

于以采蘩？于沼于沚。于以用之, 公侯之事。
于以采蘩, 于涧之中。于以用之, 公侯之宫。
被之僮僮，夙夜在公。被之祁祁，薄言还归。

Yú yǐ cǎi fán? Yú zhǎo yú zhǐ. Yú yǐ yòng zhī?
Gōng hóu zhī shì.
Yú yǐ cǎi fán, yú jiàn zhī zhōng. Yú yǐ yòng zhī?
Gōng hóu zhī gōng. Bèi zhī tóng tóng, sùyè zài gōng.
Bèi zhī qí qí, báo yán hái guī.

'WHERE do you gather the Southernwood?
Amongst the Islets, by the Pools.'
'To mingle with the other Gifts -
Such are the Prince's rules.'

There they gather in the Southernwood,
From the Streams and from the Hills.
To mingle with the Prince's Gifts
There in the Temple, which they fill.

With her Head-dress, high and stately,
Ere Dawn, in the Temple, she'll wait.
Along with her Head-dress quietly inspiring,
She'll retire to her Room, in state.

A prince's wife, in her ceremonial headdress, is inspiring to the people. The first verses set a busy scene, as the common folk decorate the temple. Then she retires, the ceremony over. Sacrifical ceremonies, presided over by the ruling classes, were important for establishing national unity.

Missing her Man

喓喓草虫，趯趯阜螽。未见君子，忧心忡忡。
亦既见止，亦既觏止，我心则降。
陟彼南山，言采其蕨。未见君子，忧心惙惙。
亦既见止，亦既觏止，我心则说。
陟彼南山，言采其薇。未见君子，我心伤悲。
亦既见止，亦既觏止，我心则夷。

Yāo yāo cǎochóng, tì tì fù zhōng.
Wèi jiàn jūnzǐ, yōuxīnchōngchōng.
Yì jì jiàn zhǐ, yì jì gòu zhǐ, wǒ xīn zé jiàng.
Zhì bǐ nánshān, yán cǎi qí jué.
Wèi jiàn jūnzǐ, yōuxīn chuò chuò.
Yì jì jiàn zhǐ, yì jì gòu zhǐ, wǒ xīn zé shuō.
Zhì bǐ nánshān, yán cǎi qí wēi.
Wèi jiàn jūnzǐ, wǒ xīn shāng bēi.
Yì jì jiàn zhǐ, yì jì gòu zhǐ, wǒ xīn zé yí.

THE CRICKETS, they chirrup, chirrup,
The Grasshoppers, they spring and fly!
But I cannot find my Man,
And stressed at Heart am I.
   O to see Him again!
   To meet Him, once again!
But I must no longer try!

Yonder I climbed the Southern Hill,
Plucking the sweet Fern as I went.
Alas my Man I still not saw,
Sadness ruined the Day I spent.
   O to see Him again!
   To meet Him, once again!
Then at last to be content!

Yonder I climbed the Southern Hill,
Plucking, as I went, the King's Fern.
Yet my Man I still not saw,
And my Heart must pine and yearn.
   O to see Him again!
   To meet Him, once again!
That our Joy might yet return!

Again a wife is missing her husband. Grasshoppers suggest late summer. Picking the ferns implies the next spring, and several months have passed. A simple heartfelt plea. The last two lines speak of meeting again!

Tile Rubbing (above) and Decorative Brick

His Pious Bride

于以采蘋？南涧之滨。于以采藻？于彼行潦。
于以盛之？维筐及筥。于以湘之？维锜及釜。
于以奠之？宗室牖下。谁其尸之？有齐季女！

Yú yǐ cǎi píng? Nán jiàn zhī bīn.
Yú yǐ cǎi zǎo? Yú bǐ xíng lǎo.
Yú yǐ shèng zhī? Wéi kuāng jí jǔ.
Yú yǐ xiāng zhī? Wéi qí jí fǔ.
Yú yǐ diàn zhī? Zōngshì yǒu xià.
Shéi qí shī zhī? Yǒu qí jì nǚ.

WHERE DID YOU gather the Water-fern?
Why, by the Streams, south of the Hills.
And where to gather the Water-grass?
By along the Roadside's swollen Rills.

And where to store what You've gathered?
Why, in shaped Baskets, round and square.
And where now to soak and simmer Them?
In the Pans and Cauldrons left out there.

Where will You go to arrange Them?
Beneath the Windows in the Hall.
And who is She there – so occupied?
Why, but our young Lord's pious Bride!

In ancient times the daughters of nobles needed to attend a service at the ancestral temple, before getting married. This song celebrates just such an occasion. The prepared plants adorn the hall, to honour the ancestral clan. Baskets, pans and cauldrons were all time-honoured utensils. As is often the case, the last lines bring the scene into sober relief.

Walking in the Dew

厌浥行露，岂不夙夜？谓行多露!
谁谓雀无角？何以穿我屋! 谁谓女无家？
何以速我狱？虽速我狱，室家不足！
谁谓鼠无牙？何以穿我墉! 谁谓女无家？
何以速我讼？虽速我讼，亦不女从!

Yàn yì xíng lù, qǐ bù sùyè? Wèi xíng duō lù!
Shéi wèi què wú jiǎo?
Héyǐ chuān wǒ wū! Shéi wèi nǚ wú jiā?
Héyǐ sù wǒ yù? Suī sù wǒ yù, shì jiā bùzú!
Shéi wèi shǔ wú yá? Héyǐ chuān wǒ yōng!
Shéi wèi nǚ wú jiā?
Héyǐ sù wǒ sòng? Suī sù wǒ sòng, yì bù nǚ cóng!

AND ALL THE PATH is soaked with Dew,
And barely day-break too?
I say, the Path is drenched with Dew!

Who says the Sparrow has no Horn?
So how breaks it into my Dwelling!
And why do You act so forlorn?

Why this forcful Compelling!
Force me, compel me, do your Will -
Husband and Wife, We will not be still!

Who says that Rats have no Teeth?
So how do they bore through my Wall!
And why do You act so forlorn?

Why force Me into this Brawl!
Force me, accuse me, even so -
I would never go with You go!

A striking piece. The drenching dew gives weight to her feelings. The man is forcing himself on the woman, that is clear. The mention of the sparrow (it steals grain) and rats (which do likewise) leave us in no doubt about the man's behaviour.

Now the Rolling Thunder

殷其雷！在南山之阳。何斯违斯，莫敢或遑？
振振君子，归哉归哉！
殷其雷！在南山之侧。何斯违斯，莫敢遑息？
振振君子，归哉归哉！
殷其雷！在南山之下。何斯违斯，莫或遑处？
振振君子，归哉归哉！

Yīnqíléi! Zài nánshān zhī yáng.
Hé sī wéi sī, mò gǎn huò huáng?
Zhèn zhèn jūnzǐ, guī zāi guī zāi!
Yīnqíléi! Zài nánshān zhī cè.
Hé sī wéi sī, mò gǎn huáng xī?
Zhèn zhèn jūnzǐ, guī zāi guī zāi!
Yīnqíléi! Zài nánshān zhī xià.
Hé sī wéi sī, mò huò huáng chù?
Zhèn zhèn jūnzǐ, guī zāi guī zāi!

LISTEN! NOW the rolling Thunder!
On Southern Hill's Crest.
Why must He then wander,
And dare not take some Rest?
Dear princely One, please, please!
Come back Home!

Listen! it's the Thunder!
Rolling o'er Southern Hill!
Why must He then wander,
Not daring to be still?
Dear princely One, please, please!
Come back Home!

Now again the Thunder!
Down there on the Plain!
So why must He then wander,
And not with me remain?
Dear princely One, please, please!
Come back Home!

Her husband is away, possibly on official duties. The binome zhenzhen (振振), 'dear princely one', is a homonym for the thunder (zhen 震), suggesting 'awe-inspiring, energetic', 'benevolent' even.

Left on the Tree

摽有梅，其实七兮。求我庶士，迨其吉兮。
摽有梅，其实三兮。求我庶士，迨其今兮。
摽有梅，顷筐墍之。求我庶士，迨其谓之。

Biāo yǒu méi, qíshí qī xī. Qiú wǒ shù shì, dài qí jí xī.
Biāo yǒu méi, qíshí sān xī. Qiú wǒ shù shì, dài qí jīn xī.
Biāo yǒu méi, qǐng kuāng jì zhī. Qiú wǒ shù shì, dài qí wèi zhī.

SHAKEN IS the damson-tree,
Yet the plums left on are seven.
You men who look at me -
You'll take any chance if given!

Shaken is the damson-tree,
Yet three plums remain still on.
You men who look at me -
Now, now! or the time is gone!

Yes, shaken is the damson-tree,
All the plums now in the basket.
Now, you men who look at me -
Please, please, the question, ask it!

The slightly humerous pleadings of an 'old maid'. As the plums ripen, more and more fall to the ground, just as she is desperate to marry.

The Emperors Concubines

嘒彼小星，三五在东。肃肃宵征，夙夜在公。寔命不同。
嘒彼小星，维参与昴。肃肃宵征，抱衾与裯。寔命不犹。

Huì bǐ xiǎo xīng, sānwǔ zài dōng. Sù sù xiāo zhēng, sùyè zài gōng. Shí mìng bùtóng.
Huì bǐ xiǎo xīng, wéi cānyù mǎo. Sù sù xiāo zhēng, bào qīn yǔ chóu. Shí mìng bù yóu.

STARLETS TINY, yonder peeping,
In the East, twice times three.
Softly, where our Lord is sleeping
Sooner or later, nightly go we.
Though not with our Lives agree.

Starlets tiny, dimly peeping,
The Pleiades, Orion's Band.
Softly, nightly We'll go creeping,
Soft-down Coverlets in the Hand.
Some higher, some lower stand.

An extraordinary song. Starlets, or merely tiny stars…suggest 'lesser wives', or concubines. The last line of each verse muses on their fate.

The Jiang has Arms

江有汜，之子归，不我以。不我以，其后也悔。
江有渚，之子归，不我与。不我与，其后也处。
江有沱，之子归，不我过。不我过，其啸也歌。

Jiāng yǒu sì, zhīzǐ guī, bù wǒ yǐ. Bù wǒ yǐ, qí hòu yě huǐ.
Jiāng yǒu zhǔ, zhīzǐ guī, bù wǒ yǔ. Bù wǒ yǔ, qí hòu yě chù.
Jiāngyǒutuó, zhīzǐ guī, bù wǒguò. Bù wǒguò, qí xiào yě gē.

THE JIANG has arms that wayward wind,
   Our Lady erstwhile his Bride.
Our Help declined –
Our Help declined,
She was of different Mind.

The Jiang has Islets within its Bed,
   Our Lady erstwhile his Bride.
Our Lands she fled -
Our Lands she fled,
And a calmer Life she led.

The Jiang has Creeks, much tangled,
   Our Lady erstwhile his Bride.
She spurned the Throng -
She spurned the Throng,
But her Haughtiness turned into Song!

The great river, the Jiang (Yangtze), is subject to its tributaries just as a monarch is subject to his people. The power of the land here` is reflected in the people. A former bride leaves a marriage. Was she abandoned, ran away, or widowed? We do not know. A voice filled with sadness yet also anger, as heard on a riverbank at dusk.

The Cedar Boat is Drifting

泛彼柏舟，亦泛其流。耿耿不寐，如有隐忧。
微我无酒，以敖以游。
我心匪鉴，不可以茹。亦有兄弟，不可以据。
薄言往愬，逢彼之怒。
我心匪石，不可转也。我心匪席，不可卷也。
威仪棣棣，不可选也。
忧心悄悄，愠于群小。觏闵既多，受侮不少。
静言思之，寤辟有摽。
日居月诸，胡迭而微？心之忧矣，如匪浣衣。
静言思之，不能奋飞。

Fàn bǐ bǎi zhōu, yì fàn qí liú. Gěnggěng bù mèi, rú yǒu yǐnyōu. Wēi wǒ wú jiǔ, yǐ áo yǐ yóu.
Wǒ xīn fěi jiàn, bùkěyǐ rú. Yì yǒu xiōngdì, bùkěyǐ jù. Báo yán wǎng sù, féng bǐ zhī nù.
Wǒ xīn fěi shí, bùkě zhuǎn yě. Wǒ xīn fěi xí, bù kě juǎn yě. Wēiyí dì dì, bù kě xuǎn yě.

Yōuxīn qiāoqiāo, yùn yú qún xiǎo. Gòu mǐn jì duō, shòu wǔ bù shǎo. Jìng yán sī zhī, wù pì yǒu biāo.
Rì jū yuè zhū, hú dié ér wēi? Xīn zhī yōu yǐ, rú fěi huǎn yī. Jìng yán sī zhī, bùnéng fènfēi.

THE CEDAR BOAT is drifting
On the Current, never still.
Sleepless I lie, and sickening,
Hit by some unknown Ill!
   It is not that Wine is wanting
   I can leave simply if I will.

My Heart is not a Mirror,
I just cannot comprehend.
Friends I have, yes, but
They are no Help in the End!
   For if I go complaining
   It is Them that I offend.

My Heart is not a Stone,
That can be turned and rolled.
My Heart not a reed Mat
That I can fold or unfold!
   Steadfast my Life has been,
   No Wrong 'gainst me can be told.

So here I sit in Sadness,
Scorned by a rabble Crew.
The Insults have been many,

My troubles not a few!
  I think 'calm down', but suddenly
  It all springs up anew!

O Moon, are you against me?
O Sun, why do you wane?
My Heart is like an old Dress
Smeared by Grief and Stain!
  I think 'calm down', then up It starts.
  I would run, but ever in vain!

A powerful song. A woman is lamenting as something has gone wrong, either in her betrothal, or her marriage. The accepted view is that she was married against her wishes. The 'rabble crew' probably refer to her in-laws.

The Scorned Wife

绿兮衣兮，绿衣黄里。心之忧矣，曷维其已！
绿兮衣兮，绿衣黄裳。心之忧矣，曷维其亡！
绿兮丝兮，女所治兮。我思古人！俾无訧兮！
絺兮绤兮，凄其以风。我思古人！实获我心！

Lǜ xī yī xī, lǜ yī huáng lǐ. Xīn zhī yōu yǐ, hé wéi qí yǐ!
Lǜ xī yī xī, lǜ yī huáng shang. Xīn zhī yōu yǐ, hé wéi qí wáng!
Lǜ xī sī xī, nǚ suǒ zhì xī. Wǒ sī gǔrén! Bǐ wú yóu xī!
Chī xī xì xī, qī qí yǐ fēng. Wǒ sī gǔrén! Shí huò wǒ xīn!

GREEN IS my Dress, green lined with yellow.
Ah! this Grief - it is not a true Fellow!

Green is the Dress, with yellow for the Skirt.
Ah! when will this Sadness cease to hurt!

Green my clothes, as guided by you.
Guide me, my Ancients! That no Harm I do!

Whatever I wear, I am chilled by the Wind.
Guide me, my Ancients! I may lose my Mind!

A women rejected by her husband; we do not know why. She thinks of the clothes he liked her to wear – and even is tempted to self-harm. But some say that the singer is actually a man, lamenting his deceased wife, and remembering the clothes she wore.

O Sun, O Moon

日居月诸，照临下土。乃如之人兮，逝不古处？
胡能有定？宁不我顾。
日居月诸，下土是冒。乃如之人兮，逝不相好。
胡能有定？宁不我报。
日居月诸，出自东方。乃如之人兮，德音无良。
胡能有定？俾也可忘。
日居月诸，东方自出。父兮母兮，畜我不卒。
胡能有定？报我不述。

Rì jū yuè zhū, zhàolín xià tǔ. Nǎi rú zhī rén xī, shì bù gǔ chù? Hú néng yǒu dìng? Níng bù wǒ gù.
Rì jū yuè zhū, xià tǔ shì mào. Nǎi rú zhī rén xī, shì bù xiānghǎo. Hú néng yǒu dìng? Níng bù wǒ bào.
Rì jū yuè zhū, chūzì dōngfāng. Nǎi rú zhī rén xī, dé yīn wú liáng. Hú néng yǒu dìng? Bǐ yě kě wàng.
Rì jū yuè zhū, dōngfāng zì chū. Fù xī mǔ xī, chù wǒ bù zú. Hú néng yǒu dìng? Bào wǒ bù shù.

O SUN, O MOON, you downward turn
To Earth your glorious Gaze.
How can there be such a Man,
Neglecting the ancient Ways!
   Can there be Peace? But no, his Glance
   Forever from me strays.

O sun, O moon, this Land below
Has you as Crown above.
How can there be such a Man,
That gives not Love for Love!
   Can there be Peace? But no, for he
   Does so ill-mannered prove.

O sun, O moon, each Morn and Eve
You climb the eastern Sky.
How can there be such a Man,
Whose Deeds fair Words belie!
   Can there be Peace? But better now
   That Memory should die!

O sun, O moon, each Morn and Eve
You rise there in the East.
O Parents mine! your Charge of me

Has never ever ceased!
 Can there be Peace? But no, for he
 Responds not in the Least.

In similar vein, a young women laments her husband's abandonment and disregard. The sun and moon are her only allies, almost acting as her real parents.

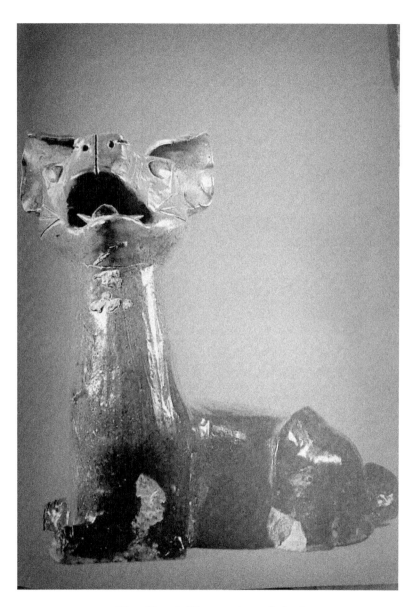

Clay Tomb Figure (watchdog)

Storm Wind

终风且暴，顾我则笑，谑浪笑敖，中心是悼。
终风且霾，惠然肯来？莫往莫来，悠悠我思。
终风且曀，不日有曀，寤言不寐，愿言则嚏。
曀曀其阴，虺虺其雷，寤言不寐，愿言则怀。

Zhōng fēng qiě bào, gù wǒ zé xiào,
Xuè làng xiào áo, zhōngxīn shì dào.
Zhōng fēng qiě mái, huì rán kěn lái?
Mò wǎng mò lái, yōuyōu wǒ sī.
Zhōng fēng qiě yì, bù rì yǒu yì,
Wù yán bù mèi, yuàn yán zé tì.
Yì yì qí yīn, huī huī qí léi,
Wù yán bù mèi, yuàn yán zé huái.

LONG, LONG the Storm Wind blew and wild,
He turned to look at me and smiled,
But Mockery was there and Scorn,
And inside my very Heart was torn!

Long, long it blew with Dust for Rain,
'Will you be kind and come again'?
He did not come, nor went his Way -
But long with many Thoughts we lay.

Still on it blows, the Storm turns Black.
Scarce Light at all, just Black on Black,
I lie awake, with starting Eyes,
And worrying Thoughts and fitful Sighs.

Black - more Black, now grows the Gloom.
Then comes the Thunder, boom, boom!
I'm still awake, any Sleep has fled -
Just heckling Thoughts inside my Head.

The misery and isolation of the spurned wife. The storm reflects her mood perfectly, such is the resonance of its lines.

Gently Blows the Valley Wind

习习谷风，以阴以雨。黾勉同心，不宜有怒。
采葑采菲，无以下体？德音莫违，及尔同死。
行道迟迟，中心有违。不远伊迩，薄送我畿。
谁谓荼苦，其甘如荠。宴尔新婚，如兄如弟。
泾以渭浊，湜湜其沚。宴尔新婚，不我屑以。
毋逝我梁，毋发我笱。我躬不阅，遑恤我后。
就其深矣，方之舟之。就其浅矣，泳之游之。
何有何亡，黾勉求之。凡民有丧，匍匐救之。
不我能慉，反以我为仇。既阻我德，贾用不售。
昔育恐育鞫，及尔颠覆。既生既育，比予于毒。
我有旨蓄，亦以御冬。宴尔新婚，以我御穷。
有洸有溃，既诒我肄。不念昔者，伊余来塈。

Xíxí gǔfēng, yǐ yīn yǐ yǔ. Miǎn miǎn tóngxīn, bùyí yǒu nù.
Cǎi fēng cǎi fēi, wú yǐxià tǐ? Dé yīn mò wéi, jí ěr tóng sǐ.
Xíngdào chí chí, zhōngxīn yǒu wéi.
Bù yuǎn yī ěr, báo sòng wǒ jī.
Shéi wèi tú kǔ, qí gān rú jì. Yàn ěr xīnhūn, rúxiōng rú dì.
Jīng yǐ wèi zhuó, shí shí qí zhǐ.

Yàn ěr xīnhūn, bù wǒ xiè yǐ.
Wú shì wǒ liáng, wú fā wǒ gǒu. Wǒ gōng bù yuè, huáng xù wǒ hòu.
Jiù qí shēn yǐ, fāngzhīzhōu zhī.
Jiù qí qiǎn yǐ, yǒng zhī yóu zhī.
Hé yǒu hé wáng, miǎn miǎn qiú zhī. Fán mínyǒu sàng, púfú jiù zhī.
Bù wǒ néng xù, fǎn yǐ wǒ wèi chóu.
Jì zǔ wǒ dé, jiǎ yòng bù shòu.
Xī yù kǒng yù jū, jí ěr diānfù. Jì shēng jì yù, bǐ yǔ yú dú.
Wǒ yǒu zhǐ xù, yì yǐ yù dōng.
Yàn ěr xīnhūn, yǐ wǒ yù qióng.
Yǒu guāng yǒu kuì, jì yí wǒ yì. Bù niàn xī zhě, yī yú lái jì.

GENTLY, GENTLY blows the Valley Wind,
Bringing Clouds of Gloom and Rain.
Once We strove together in Heart,
And angry Thoughts We would restrain.
When we gathered Mustard, or Melon
We'd leave the Roots untouched beneath.
Do you reject me now, my moral Tone?
We were to live together until Death.

With slow, slow Steps I took to the Road
My innermost Heart retreating.
You barely saw me to the Door,
No distance at all, for all my pleading.
Who calls the Sow-thistle bitter?
Like the Water-cress it's just as sweet.
You feast there with your new Bride,
'Good-natured' as when Family meet.

The River Jing is made muddy by the Wei,
But in its Shoals it will turn clear.
You feast there with your new Bride.
And think me not worth coming near.
Don't come by my Fish-dam!
Don't You touch my Nets!

41

Everything of mine you've thrown away,
In a hurry to forget your Regrets.

Where the River ran wide and deep
On a Raft or Boat I'd paddle o'er,
But where it ran shallower
I'd dive and swim to the Shore.
What We had and what We lost,
I'd strained every Nerve to find.
While when Others had Troubles, I'd go
And give them my All, and be kind.

Now you show me no loving Care.
 I'm treated as Enemy, and you tell
How my Virtue stood in your Way,
Like market Goods that will not sell.
Once We feared we might not live -
But in your Downturn I shared.
Yet now, when Fortune smiles on you,
To Poison I am compared!

I had laid down a plentiful Store,
Of good Food for the Winter to be.
Feast on it then, with your young Bride,
It was thus I that eased your Poverty.

The Water glitters, dashing on the rocks,
In the end it comforts my Pain.
You have forgotten All that went before,
But for me happy Thoughts remain.

A grand opus! This is a classic 'he done me wrong' song. At first she feels bitter. But in the last two lines of the last verse a ray of sunlight appears, as she meditates on the tumbling waters of the river. The whole narrative shows the great power of Daoist acceptance.

Those Spring Waters

毖彼泉水，亦流于淇。有怀于卫，靡日不思。
娈彼诸姬，聊与之谋。
出宿于泲，饮饯于祢，女子有行，远父母兄弟。
问我诸姑，遂及伯姊。
出宿于干，饮饯于言。载脂载舝，还车言迈。
遄臻于卫，不瑕有害？
我思肥泉，兹之永叹。思须与漕，我心悠悠。
驾言出游，以写我忧。

Bì bǐ quánshuǐ, yì liú yú qí. Yǒu huái yú wèi, mí rì bù sī.
Luán bǐ zhū jī, liáo yǔ zhī móu.
Chū sù yú jǐ, yǐn jiàn yú mí, nǚzǐ yǒu xíng, yuǎn fùmǔ xiōngdì.
Wèn wǒ zhū gū, suì jí bó zǐ.
Chū sù yú gàn, yǐn jiàn yú yán. Zài zhī zài xiá, hái chē yán mài.
Chuán zhēn yú wèi, bù xiá yǒuhài?
Wǒ sī féi quán, zī zhī yǒng tàn. Sī xū yǔ cáo, wǒ xīn yōuyōu.
Jià yán chūyóu, yǐ xiè wǒ yōu.

THOSE SPRING WATERS, running so free,
Are straight from the Source of the River Qi.
But my Heart, it lies still in the State of Wei,
And I cannot forget it – every Day.
   For there are my Cousins, those of my kin.
   And I should call and counsel with Them.

When I left Home, I was lodged at Ji,
And we drank the Marriage-cup at Ni.
A married Woman leaves behind All,
With no Brothers, Sisters or Family to call.
   Could You but let me my Aunts to meet,
   I'd go forward then, my Sisters to greet.

And leaving here I could lodge at Gan,
And stop for some Refreshment at Yan.
We could grease the Axle, mount back in,
And pass through all the Places I'd been.
   Soon we'd arrive at Wei, but no –
   Surely I am wrong to think thus so!

I'm awake, thinking of Fei and its Streams,
And lie a long Time, seeing it in my Dreams.

And I remember Xu, and also Cao...
My Heart being full enough to overflow!
  If I were there! the Journey to undertake...
  This Yearning then I could forsake!

According to the Han dynasty Mao Preface a 'young girl marries, her parents die and she longs to return home'. A common theme. Ji and Ni were towns she passed through on her wedding journey. This song express her intense grief and longing for her homeland and family (but see note to Song 54). Note the opening lines – how she envies the free-running spring waters.

Past The New Tower

新台有泚，河水弥弥。燕婉之求，籧篨不鲜。
新台有洒，河水浼浼。燕婉之求，籧篨不殄。
鱼网之设，鸿则离之。燕婉之求，得此戚施。

Xīntái yǒu cǐ, héshuǐ mí mí. Yàn wǎn zhī qiú, qú chú bù xiān.
Xīntái yǒu sǎ, héshuǐ měi měi. Yàn wǎn zhī qiú, qú chú bù tiǎn.
Yúwǎng zhī shè, hóng zé lí zhī. Yàn wǎn zhī qiú, dé cǐ qī shī.

PAST THE NEW TOWER, shining bright,
Flows the River He, its Waters murky.
I was looking for some handsome Fellow,
But found this Character, one old and dirty!

Under the New Tower, lofty and high,
Run the Waters of the River He, so still.
I was looking for some handsome Fellow,
But found this Bloke, a downright Imbecile!

It was a Fish-net that I thought to set,
But a stupid Goose came along instead!
I was looking for some handsome Fellow,
But it turned out a misshapen Brute I wed!

The New Tower was built by the Emperor Wei Xuangong, (ruled 718-700 BCE). He was so enamoured of his son's young wife, Xuan Jiang that he took her for himself. The story is that she was incarcerated in this newly-build tower, on imperial grounds. See song 46.

Our Two Boys

二子乘舟，泛泛其景。愿言思子，中心养养！
二子乘舟，泛泛其逝。愿言思子，不瑕有害！

Èrzi chéng zhōu, fànfàn qí jǐng. Yuàn yán sī zǐ, zhōngxīn yǎng yǎng!
Èrzi chéng zhōu, fànfàn qí shì. Yuàn yán sī zǐ, bù xiá yǒu hài!

OUR TWO BOYS went off in a Boat,
The Water was still as a Gem.
But I fear for you, my Lads, so young,
My Heart now is all in a Spin!

Our two Boys went off in a Boat,
They floated far out into the Stream.
But I fear for you, my Lads, so young,
Do They deserve to come to Harm!

There is clear agreement among commentators that these two boys were sons of Wei Xuangong (see last song), but from different wives. Because of the jealousy between his heirs, the Emperor plotted their demise and both were murdered. This was to sow the seed of infighting, intrigue and murder for several future generations!

Little She Understands Me

泛彼柏舟，在彼中河。髧彼两髦，实维我仪。
之死矢靡它。母也天只！不谅人只！
泛彼柏舟，在彼河侧。髧彼两髦，实维我特。
之死矢靡慝。母也天只！不谅人只！

Fàn bǐ bǎi zhōu, zài bǐ zhōng hé. Dàn bǐ liǎng máo, shí wéi wǒ yí.
Zhī sǐ shǐ mí tā. Mǔ yě tiān zhǐ! Bù liàng rén zhǐ!
Fàn bǐ bǎi zhōu, zài bǐ hé cè. Dàn bǐ liǎng máo, shí wéi wǒ tè.
Zhī sǐ shǐ mí tè. Mǔ yě tiān zhǐ! Bù liàng rén zhǐ!

DIPPING UNSTEADILY, that Boat of Yew,
Lies midway upon the River He.
That Boy with twin front Locks, I knew -
Was my rightful Mate - and till Death
I vowed None else to know.
   My Mother, kind as Heaven is she!
   But O, little She understands me!

Dipping unsteadily, that Boat of Yew,
Is now by the River's Brim.
That Boy with twin front Locks I knew –
One only – and I vowed to do
Till Death, no wrong to him.
   My Mother, kind as Heaven is she!
   But O, little She understands me!

   A young girl's concern, resentment even, at not getting her mother's consent about the boy she wishes to marry. Twin locks of hair mean he had not yet reached twenty. The hair was cut at maturity (or else on the death of his parents). The dipping, unsteady boat reflects her mental state.

On the Wall a Thorn Bush

墙有茨，不可扫也。中冓之言，不可道也。
所可道也，言之丑也。
墙有茨，不可襄也。中冓之言，不可详也。
所可详也，言之长也。
墙有茨，不可束也。中冓之言，不可读也。
所可读也，言之辱也。

Qiáng yǒu cí, bùkě sǎo yě. Zhōng gòu zhī yán, bùkě dào yě.
Suǒ kě dào yě, yán zhī chǒu yě.
Qiáng yǒu cí, bùkě xiāng yě. Zhōng gòu zhī yán, bùkě xiáng yě.
Suǒ kě xiáng yě, yán zhī cháng yě.
Qiáng yǒu cí, bùkě shù yě. Zhōng gòu zhī yán, bùkě dú yě.
Suǒ kě dú yě, yán zhī rǔ yě.

ON THE WALL A THORN bush clambers,
No fencing will ever take hold.
And the tale of my lady's chambers
Is such as may never be told.
   What might be told
   Would the vilest scene unfold.

On the wall a thorn bush clambers,
It cannot be got rid of well.
And the tale of my lady's chambers,
On it one never should dwell.
   On it to dwell,
   Would be a weary tale to tell.

On the wall a thorn bush clambers,
Who'll bind and drag it away?
And the tale of my lady's chambers
Who'll dare to sing out or say?
   And to sing out or say,
   Would be a shameful lay.

Another song with a story behind it. After the death of Emperor Wei (see Song 43) a son from a former marriage was forced to marry his step-mother, the lady Xuan Jiang, 'in order to consolidate the rule'. However

54

there is strong evidence that they had been intimate before the Emperor's death. The lines show the people's disgust and shame at such behaviour.

A Ruler's Wife

君子偕老，副笄六珈。委委佗佗，如山如河，象服是宜。
子之不淑，云如之何！
玼兮玼兮，其之翟也。鬒发如云，不屑髢也；
玉之瑱也，象之揥也，扬且之皙也。胡然而天也！
胡然而帝也？
瑳兮瑳兮，其之展也！蒙彼绉絺，是绁袢也。
子之清扬，扬且之颜也。展如之人兮，邦之媛也！

Jūnzǐ xiélǎo, fù jī liù jiā. Wěi wěi tuó tuó, rúshān rú hé, xiàng fú shì yí.
Zǐ zhī bù shū, yún rú zhī hé!
Cǐ xī cǐ xī, qí zhī dí yě. Zhěn fā rú yún, bùxiè dí yě;
yù zhī zhèn yě, xiàng zhī tì yě, yáng qiě zhī xī yě. Hú rán'ér tiān yě! Hú rán'ér dì yě?
Cuō xī cuō xī, qí zhī zhǎn yě! Méng bǐ zhòu chī, shì xiè pàn yě.
Zǐ zhī qīng yáng, yáng qiě zhī yán yě. Zhǎn rú zhī rén xī, bāngzhī yuàn yě!

A RULER'S WIFE, to end of her Life!
See her, the queenly Head-dress wear –
Six Pins jewelled in her Hair.
What Elegance! what Grace there!
   As of Nature's Hills and Rills.
   And yes, the Dress her Body fills!
Yet with all her Virtues amiss,
Why needs She the like of this!

How rich and fair, rich and rare!
In festal Robe, the pheasant Plumes!
And her black Hair, like a Cloud it looms!
False Locks she scorns, nor even assumes.
Of precious Stone her Ear-plugs are,
   A Comb of Ivor y binds her Hair,
   A lofty Forehead, so white and fair!
Ah! appearing celestial, is she –
Who does She think she is! a Deity?

How splendidly, how brilliantly
Her Robes of Ceremony shine!
Worn over Crepe and Lawn so fine,
As with her Warmth the Whole combine.

Arched her Brows and bright the Eyes,
And broadly full her Temples rise.
Ah! what a Woman! to stand
As if she were the Fairest in the Land!

These 'catty' lines make it clear this lady's demeanour is unwelcome. Chinese commentaries think this is a sharp satire aimed at Xuan Jiang (see the previous song where the suspicion is she took to bed her half-brother, the son of her late husband by a former wife), and the people were outraged. Her fine clothing and attire did not match her morals.

Quails Consort

鹑之奔奔，鹊之强强。人之无良，我以为兄！
鹊之强强，鹑之奔奔。人之无良，我以为君！

Chún zhī bēn bēn, què zhī qiáng qiáng.
Rén zhī wú liáng, wǒ yǐwéi xiōng!
Què zhī qiáng qiáng, chún zhī bēn bēn.
Rén zhī wú liáng, wǒ yǐwéi jūn!

QUAILS CONSORT and fly with Quails,
Jays will solely join with Jays.
So I own him as an elder Brother
Despite him taking to wanton Ways.

Jay will only have his Jay,
While Quail goes with consort Quail.
One who's taken to wanton Ways
Must I now still as 'My Lord' hail.

Her husband has fallen for another woman. Yet she stands by him, despite his unscrupulous behaviour. Indeed her bitterness lets her see he has finally caught up with his own kind. Birds of a feather flock together. Some commentators link this to the events described in the last two songs.

Forth Must I Gallop

载驰载驱，归唁卫侯！
驱马悠悠，言至于漕。大夫跋涉，我心则忧。
既不我嘉，不能旋反。视尔不臧，我思不远。
既不我嘉，不能旋济？视尔不臧，我思不閟。
陟彼阿丘，言采其蝱。女子善怀！
亦各有行。许人尤之！众稚且狂！
我行其野，芃芃其麦。控于大邦，谁因谁极？
大夫君子，无我有尤。百尔所思，不如我所之。

Zài chí zài qū, guī yàn wèi hóu! Qū mǎ yōuyōu, yán zhìyú cáo. Dàfū báshè, wǒ xīn zé yōu.
Jì bù wǒ jiā, bùnéng xuán fǎn. Shì ěr bù zāng, wǒ sī bù yuǎn.
Jì bù wǒ jiā, bùnéng xuán jì? Shì ěr bù zāng, wǒ sī bù bì.
Zhì bǐ ā qiū, yán cǎi qí méng. Nǚzǐ shàn huái! Yì gè yǒu xíng.
Xǔrényóu zhī! Zhòng zhì qiě kuáng!
Wǒ xíng qí yě, péng péng qí mài. Kòng yú dà bāng, shéi yīn shéi jí?
Dàfū jūnzǐ, wú wǒ yǒu yóu. Bǎi ěr suǒ sī, bùrú wǒ suǒ zhī.

FORTH MUST I GALLOP and Homeward fly!
To cheer in their Troubles the lords of Wei.
And urging my Horses onward all Day,
I can reach Cao City with no Delay.
Like a Courier I can cross Rivers and Plains,
As my Heart immersed in Sorrow remains.
But my Pleasures, it seems, are not your own,
And any Hope of Return is overthrown.
Yet though it is clear You disapprove,
My passionate Mind no Power can move.

My Pleasures are not your own, it seems,
But can I not return and re-cross the Streams?
I know that You disapprove, that's plain -
But the passionate Mind none can restrain.
I will climb to the Top of the Great Mound,
Where the Mother-of-pearl Lilies are found.
We Women are full of Needs, they say!
But every want must have its way.
And wrong you are ! You men of Xu!
Childish and headstrong, that is you!

I'd travel across any wide, wide Plain
Now clad in its richly-waving Grain.
And carry my Case before any great State,
For whatever Cause – if the Need were great!
Now you so-called Officers, of high Degree,
Say not that the Error lies with me.
For the Counsels of you all combined
Will be nowhere near what I have in Mind!

This splendid song was penned by Lady Xumu (许穆夫人) the first identifiable woman poet in Chinese history. It cannot have originated much later than 670 BCE. Her authorship has also been linked to Song 39 Spring Waters and 59 Thoughts of Home. She was a Wei princess married to the Lord of Xu in 671 BCE

When Wei state was conquered she felt she had to return to her own Land. The officers who detained her are from Xu. I've used a galloping metre.

An 'Honest Fellow'

氓之蚩蚩，抱布贸丝。匪来贸丝，来即我谋。
　　　　送子涉淇，至于顿丘。
匪我愆期，子无良媒？将子无怒，秋以为期。
乘彼垝垣，以望复关。不见复关，泣涕涟涟。
　　　　既见复关，载笑载言。
尔卜尔筮，体无咎言。以尔车来，以我贿迁。
桑之未落，其叶沃若。于嗟鸠兮！无食桑葚。
　　　　于嗟女兮！无与士耽。
士之耽兮，犹可说也。女之耽兮，不可说也。
桑之落矣，其黄而陨。自我徂尔，三岁食贫。
　　　　淇水汤汤，渐车帷裳。
女也不爽，士贰其行。士也罔极，二三其德。
三岁为妇，靡室劳矣。夙兴夜寐，靡有朝矣。
　　　　言既遂矣，至于暴矣。

Máng zhī chī chī, bào bù mào sī. Fěi lái mào sī, lái jí wǒ móu. Sòng zi shè qí, zhìyú dùn qiū.
Fěi wǒ qiānqí, zǐ wú liáng méi? Jiāng zǐ wú nù, qiū yǐwéi qī.

Chéng bǐ guǐ yuán, yǐ wàng fù guān. Bùjiàn fù guān, qì tì lián lián. Jì jiàn fù guān, zài xiào zài yán.
Ěr bo ěr shì, tǐ wú jiù yán. Yǐ ěr chē lái, yǐ wǒ huì qiān.
Sāng zhī wèi luò, qí yè wò ruò. Yú jiē jiū xī! Wú shí sāngrèn.
Yú jiē nǚ xī! Wú yǔ shì dān.
Shì zhī dān xī, yóu kě shuō yě. Nǚ zhī dān xī, bùkě shuō yě.
Sāng zhī luò yǐ, qí huáng ér yǔn. Zìwǒ cú ěr, sān suì shí pín.
Qí shuǐ tāng tāng, jiàn chē wéi shang.
Nǚ yě bùshuǎng, shì èr qí xíng. Shì yě wǎng jí, èrsān qí dé.
Sān suì wèi fù, mí shì láo yǐ. Sù xīng yè mèi, mí yǒu zhāo yǐ.
Yán jìsuì yǐ, zhìyú bào yǐ.
Xiōngdì bùzhī, xì qí xiào yǐ. Jìng yán sī zhī, gōng zì dào yǐ.
Jí ěr xiélǎo, lǎo shǐ wǒ yuàn. Qí zé yǒu àn, xí zé yǒu pàn.
Zǒng jiǎo zhī yàn, yánxiào yàn yàn, xìnshìdàndàn, bù sī qí fǎn. Fǎn shì bù sī, yì yǐ yān zāi!

AN HONEST FELLOW you did seem,
Peddling Cloth, for Thread to sell.
But It were no such Thing –
For to catch me was your Plan to tell.
  ' Would I cross with you the River Qi?
   Would I follow you as far as Dunqui?'
'I would not delay', I cried,
But with no Match-maker, no Bride'?
'No, do not get mad'! I said.
'Let's wait 'til Harvest-tide, instead'.

Those broken, ruined Walls I'd climb
For a Glimpse of far Fuguan.
And when Fuguan I could not see
My Tears would fall incessantly.
   Then You arrived! And oh...
   How We would laugh and talk so!
You would question the Stalks and Shell.
'Nothing wrong', You said. 'All's well!'
So with your Wagon You had come,
To take me off to your Home.

Before the Mulberry sheds its Leaves,
Fresh and fair They are to see.

Ah thou! my littlest Dove,
Do not eat the Fruit of that Tree!
  Ah thou! my sweet Lady,
  Do not with him be so free!
When a Man indulges at his whim
Much can be said to excuse him.
But when a Woman does the same,
Ne'er can She escape the Blame!

Just as the Mulberry drops its Leaves,
They tumble yellow from the Tree.
Since I have gone along with you,
We've had three Years of Poverty.
  My Tears! as if the full Waters of River Qi
  Have soaked my Carriage curtain's screen!
N'er a lack of Heart in me,
But two Faces in you are all I see.
At any turn of Luck you've faltered,
And so an honest Course is altered.

Three years I lived with you as Wife,
Of household Toil I never cared,
Rising early, and late to Bed
Not a single Day I spared.

So the Part was fulfilled by me -
   But then began your Cruelty.
My Brothers they did not know this,
They'd shout and laugh at me.
So on my own quiet Thoughts I'm thrown
And know I must face this alone.

'Bound together till old Age', they say -
But Age to me, Discord brings.
Just as by the edge of the River Qi are held
Its more swampy Marshes and Springs.
   In younger, happier Days, I'd wear
   My Hair in a Knot, We'd talk and laugh.
Daily truthful to that Vow,
Never dreamt of it to disallow.
Thoughts of It broken? I've had none.
Ah 'tis me! Undone! undone!

   A heart-breaking tale. Fuguan is the province where the peddlar originated from.

Thoughts of Home

籊籊竹竿，以钓于淇。岂不尔思？远莫致之。
泉源在左，淇水在右。女子有行，远兄弟父母。
淇水在右，泉源在左。巧笑之瑳，佩玉之傩。
淇水滺滺，桧楫松舟！驾言出游！以写我忧！

Tì tì zhúgān, yǐ diào yú qí. Qǐ bù ěr sī? Yuǎn mò zhì zhī.
Quányuán zài zuǒ, qí shuǐ zài yòu. Nǚzǐ yǒu xíng, yuǎn xiōngdì fùmǔ.
Qí shuǐ zài yòu, quányuán zài zuǒ. Qiǎo xiào zhī cuō, pèiyù zhī nuó.
Qí shuǐ yōu yōu, guì jí sōng zhōu! Jià yán chūyóu! Yǐ xiě wǒ yōu!

WITH LONG and slender Rods of Bamboo,
We used to go Fishing by the River Qi.
Now my Thoughts are returning to You -
But You are far away, Impossible to see.

To the Left run the bubbling Springs,
To the Right, the River Qi.
A Girl married must leave her Kin -
Her Family then will distant be.

To the Right, the River Qi,
To the Left, run bubbling Springs.
Their sweet laughs, I still seem to see,
Their tinkling Gems on girdle Strings....

Ah, may the swift Waters carry onward
My Boat of Pine, with its Oars of Yew!
O, to travel in my Carriage with them!
That then my Sorrows might be few!

Sung by a country-girl, married and taken to foreign parts. Her thoughts stray back her friends from younger days. Poignant and full of feeling. But see note to Song 54. Probably from the same pen.

Young Lad

芄兰之支，童子佩觿。虽则佩觿，能不我知。
容兮遂兮，垂带悸兮。
芄兰之叶，童子佩韘。虽则佩韘，能不我甲。
容兮遂兮，垂带悸兮。

Wán lán zhī zhī, tóngzǐ pèi xī. Suīzé pèi xī, néng bù wǒ zhī.
Róng xī suì xī, chuí dài jì xī.
Wán lán zhī yè, tóngzǐ pèi shè. Suīzé pèi shè, néng bù wǒ jiǎ.
Róng xī suì xī, chuí dài jì xī.

ON THE SPARROW-gourd, Buds begin to show
And at the young Lad's Belt, a Bodkin seen!
A Bodkin has at his Girdle been,
But of us, that Boy can nothing know.
   What smug Conceit, what swaggering Air!
   Him with a Bodkin at his Girdle, dangling
      there!

The Sparrow-gourd is just coming into Leaf,
And at the Lad's Waist, an archer's Ring!
Let him wear at his Waist an archer's Ring,
But among us that Boy will never be Chief.
   What smug Conceit, what swaggering Air!
   Him with a Ring at his Girdle, dangling
      there!

Bodkin, a pin used for loosening knots. Archer's ring, a thumb ring, for drawing back the bow-string. The lines ridicule the lad's posturing, and immaturity.

Away at the Wars

伯兮朅兮，邦之桀兮。伯也执殳，为王前驱。
自伯之东，首如飞蓬。岂无膏沐？谁适为容！
其雨其雨，杲杲出日。愿言思伯，甘心首疾。
焉得谖草？言树之背。愿言思伯。使我心痗。

Bó xī qiè xī, bāngzhī jié xī.
Bó yě zhí shū, wèi wáng qiánqū.
Zì bó zhī dōng, shǒu rú fēipéng.
Qǐ wú gāo mù? Shéi shì wèi róng!
Qí yǔ qí yǔ, gǎo gǎo chū rì.
Yuàn yán sī bó, gānxīn shǒu jí.
Yān dé xuān ǎo? Yán shù zhī bèi.
Yuàn yán sīc bó. Shǐ wǒ xīn mèi.

MY LORD, a proper Man is he,
The Hero of this Land.
Before his King he has galloped off
With Spear and Lance in hand.

Since East he went, my Hair's undone
It flies flax-like in the Breeze.
Maybe I'll dress and tidy it up -
But Who is there to please?

'We need Rain, Rain!', yet still the Sun
Comes up to a cloudless Sky.
I must think on my Lord, brave Heart -
But my Head is too sore to try!

Oh, for the Herb that Memory kills,
That I may plant it beside my Wall.
Yet these thoughts of my Lord, brave Heart,
Are anguish to us all!

The background to this song is war. The first stanza sets the scene as her husband rushes off. The atmosphere builds, until, in the last line, her pain and suffering burst through. A telling piece.

There, That Lone Fox

有狐绥绥，在彼淇梁。心之忧矣，之子无裳。
有狐绥绥，在彼淇厉。心之忧矣，之子无带。
有狐绥绥，在彼淇侧。心之忧矣，之子无服。

Yǒu hú suí suí, zài bǐ qí liáng. Xīn zhī yōu yǐ, zhīzǐ wú shang.
Yǒu hú suí suí, zài bǐ qí lì. Xīn zhī yōu yǐ, zhīzǐ wú dài.
Yǒu hú suí suí, zài bǐ qí cè. Xīn zhī yōu yǐ, zhīzǐ wú fú.

THERE, THAT LONE FOX, so forlorn;
There by the Dam o'er the River Qi.
That Man, his ragged Clothing, all torn!
A dismal Sight is he to me.

There, that Lone Fox, so forlorn;
There by the Ford cross the River Qi.
That Man, his Dress all ragged, torn!
A dismal Sight is he to me.

There, that Lone Fox, so forlorn;
There by the Bank of the River Qi.
That Man, his Leggings all ragged, torn!
A dismal Sight is he to me.

Aloneness during a time of war and turmoil. A woman, possibly widowed, yearns for companionship. The original text is very concise and I have tried to copy this in translation.

My Old Man Has Marching Gone

君子于役，不知其期，曷至哉？
鸡栖于埘，日之夕矣，羊牛下来。
君子于役，如之何勿思！
君子于役，不日不月，曷其有佸？
鸡栖于桀，日之夕矣，羊牛下括。
君子于役，苟无饥渴！

Jūnzǐ yú yì, bùzhī qí qī, hé zhì zāi?
Jī qī yú shí, rì zhī xī yǐ, yáng niú xiàlái.
Jūnzǐ yú yì, rú zhī hé wù sī!
Jūnzǐ yú yì, bù rì bù yuè, hé qí yǒu huó?
Jī qī yú jié, rì zhī xī yǐ, yáng niú xià kuò.
Jūnzǐ yú yì, gǒu wú jī kě!

MY OLD MAN has Marching gone,
Not knowing when his Term will end.
But where is He lodging now?
   The Fowls go back to their Perches
   At the Evening of the Day.
   And Goats and Cattle come down the Hill,
But my old Man has gone marching away.
   How can I stop thinking of him!

My old Man has Marching gone,
We do not know how many Days!
And when will I see again?
   The Fowls go back to their Perches
   At the Evening of the Day.
   And Goats and Cattle come down apace,
But my old Man has gone marching away.
   Might he never know hunger or thirst!

Missing her husband, who is away at the wars. This song has an evocative, rural nature.

Troubles in the Vale

中谷有蓷，暵其乾矣。有女仳离。
嘅其叹矣，嘅其叹矣，遇人之艰难矣！
中谷有蓷，暵其修矣。有女仳离。
条其啸矣，条其啸矣，遇人之不淑矣！
中谷有蓷，暵其湿矣。有女仳离。
啜其泣矣，啜其泣矣，何嗟及矣！

Zhōnggǔ yǒu tuī, hàn qí qián yǐ. Yǒu nǚ pǐ lí.
Kǎi qí tàn yǐ, kǎi qí tàn yǐ, yù rén zhī jiānnán yǐ!
Zhōnggǔ yǒu tuī, hàn qí xiū yǐ. Yǒu nǚ pǐ lí.
Tiáo qí xiào yǐ, tiáo qí xiào yǐ, yù rén zhī bù shū yǐ!
Zhōnggǔ yǒu tuī, hàn qí shī yǐ. Yǒu nǚ pǐ lí.
Chuài qí qì yǐ, chuài qí qì yǐ, hé jiē jí yǐ!

DEEP IN THE VALE the Motherwort grows,
But it is parched on the waterless Ground.
This is a Woman forced apart from her Man,
  Ah, hear her Cry!
  Ah, hear her Cry!
She suffers the Troubles he found.

Deep in the Vale the Motherwort grows,
But it is parched where once It grew Tall.
This is a Woman forced apart from her Man,
  With drawn-out Moan!
  With drawn-out Moan!
Upon them both, his Misfortunes fall.

Deep in the Vale the Motherwort grows,
But it is parched in Places once wet.
This is a Woman forced apart from her Man,
  Her Tears running down!
  Her Tears running down!
But more Trouble is coming yet!

A woman has been forced apart from her husband, for whatever reason, we do not know. The sonorous tone of the whole song echoes the failing motherwort.

The Wife's Affection

彼采葛兮，一日不见，如三月兮！
彼采萧兮，一日不见，如三秋兮！
彼采艾兮！一日不见，如三岁兮！

Bǐ cǎi gé xī, yī rì bùjiàn, rú sān yuè xī!
Bǐ cǎi xiāo xī, yī rì bùjiàn, rú sānqiū xī!
Bǐ cǎi ài xī! Yī rì bùjiàn, rú sān suì xī!

THERE HE IS, gathering the Creeper!
Only one Day away from him,
And it is like three Months to me!

There He is, picking the Southern-grass!
Only one Day away from him,
And three Autumns seem to pass!

There He is, it's the Mugwort he clears!
Only one Day away from him,
And it seems like three Years!

A simple song. Its powerful human emotion has passed through the dust of generations into our hearts. For this on its own we should be grateful.

The Grand Carriage

大车槛槛，毳衣如菼。岂不尔思？畏子不敢！
大车啍啍，毳衣如璊。岂不尔思？畏子不奔。
榖则异室，死则同穴。谓予不信，有如皎日！

Dà chē kǎn kǎn, cuì yī rú tǎn. Qǐ bù ěr sī? Wèi zi bù gǎn!
Dà chē tūn tūn, cuì yī rú mén. Qǐ bù ěr sī? Wèi zi bù bēn.
Gǔ zé yì shì, sǐ zé tóng xué. Wèi yú bùxìn, yǒurú jiǎo rì!

THE GRAND CARRIAGE - how it thunders!
Your furred, green-emblazoned Robes there!
Did you wonder I might have forgotten you?
  But I am in Awe, and do not dare!

The grand Carriage - how it rumbles!
Your fine-furred, dark-red Robes alight!
Did you wonder I might have forgotten you?
  But I am in Awe, with no Thought of Flight.

In Life we might live in separate Houses,
But at Death, in the same Grave We'll lie!
Now You have said that I am Faithless?
  I am not! by the bright Sun in the Sky!

A simple love-song, written by a girl about her man. She seems intimidated by his wealth, and appearance. But she vehemently reaffirms her eternal devotion. Some commentators believe actually it is a woman in the carriage, with the singer a man.

Loitering Still

丘中有麻，彼留子嗟。彼留子嗟，将其来施施。
丘中有麦，彼留子国。彼留子国，将其来食。
丘中有李，彼留之子。彼留之子，贻我佩玖。

Qiū zhōng yǒu má, bǐ liú zi jiē. Bǐ liú zi jiē, jiāng qí lái shī shī.
Qiū zhōng yǒu mài, bǐ liú zǐ guó. Bǐ liú zǐ guó, jiāng qí lái shí.
Qiū zhōng yǒu lǐ, bǐ liú zhīzǐ. Bǐ liú zhīzǐ, yí wǒ pèi jiǔ.

AMONG the Hemp up on the Hill,
   Zijie is loitering still.
   Zijie is loitering still -
Would He but come and talk to me.

Among the Wheat up on the Hill,
   Ziguo is loitering still.
   Ziguo is loitering still -
Would He but come and eat with me.

Among the Plum-trees on the Hill,
   Those two Boys are loitering still.
   Those two Boys are loitering still –
Each could give me a Gem for my Girdle!

A charming piece. Note how the last line brings into sharp focus the girl's interest in getting to know these boys better.

His Jet-black Robes

缁衣之宜兮！敝予又改为兮。适子之馆兮，还予授子之粲兮。
缁衣之好兮！敝予又改造兮。适子之馆兮，还予授子之粲兮。
缁衣之席兮！敝予又改作兮。适子之馆兮，还予授子之粲兮。

Zī yī zhī yí xī! Bì yǔ yòu gǎi wèi xī. Shì zǐ zhī guǎn xī, hái yǔ shòu zǐ zhī càn xī.
Zī yī zhī hǎo xī! Bì yǔ yòu gǎizào xī. Shì zǐ zhī guǎn xī, hái yǔ shòu zǐ zhī càn xī.
Zī yī zhī xí xī! Bì yǔ yòu gǎizuò xī. Shì zǐ zhī guǎn xī, hái yǔ shòu zǐ zhī càn xī.

O HIS JET-BLACK Robes, how becoming!
And when worn out, I've others I'll prepare.
And when the Lodges our Prince will attend,
Returning, a Feast for him I'll send.

O his jet-black Robes, how ornate and grand!
And when worn out, I'll have others at hand.
And when the Lodges our Prince will attend,
Returning, a Feast for him I'll send.

O the jet-black Robes, his Figure they grace!
And when outworn More will be in place.
And when the Lodges our Prince will attend,
Returning, a Feast for him I'll send.

The powerful image of the jet-black robes shows the grand importance given to clothing and etiquette in the ancient court. Obviously a family with influence. A snapshot of life among the old Chinese gentry.

Master Zhong, I Pray you

将仲子兮, 无逾我里, 无折我树杞! 岂敢爱之, 畏我父母?
仲可怀也, 父母之言亦可畏也!
将仲子兮, 无逾我墙, 无折我树桑。岂敢爱之, 畏我诸兄?
仲可怀也, 诸兄之言亦可畏也!
将仲子兮, 无逾我园, 无折我树檀。岂敢爱之? 畏人之多言。
仲可怀也, 人之多言亦可畏也!

Jiāng zhòngzi xī, wú yú wǒ lǐ, wú zhé wǒ shù qǐ!
Qǐgǎn ài zhī, wèi wǒ fùmǔ?
Zhòng kě huái yě, fùmǔ zhī yán yì kě wèi yě!
Jiāng zhòngzi xī, wú yú wǒ qiáng, wú zhé wǒ shù sāng.
Qǐgǎn ài zhī, wèi wǒ zhū xiōng?
Zhòng kě huái yě, zhū xiōng zhī yán yì kě wèi yě!
Jiāng zhòngzi xī, wú yú wǒ yuán, wú zhé wǒ shù tán.
Qǐgǎn ài zhī? Wèi rén zhī duō yán.
Zhòng kě huái yě, rén zhī duō yán yì kě wèi yě!

MASTER ZHONG, I PRAY YOU, please,
Don't' break down our Willow-trees!
Don't come prancing through our Village.
   Not that I particularly care for them,
   But what might my Parents think ?
Zhong, you are a likable Chap,
But what will my Parents think?
That could be truly Awful!

Master Zhong, please don't sprawl,
Don't' jump like that over our Wall!
Don't break through the Mulberries.
   Not that I particularly care for them,
   But what might my Brothers say?
Zhong, you are a good Sort,
But what will my Brothers say?
That could be truly Awful!

Master Zhong, it were better not
You come bounding into our Plot,
And disturbing our Sandal-trees!
   Not that I particularly care for them,
   But I fear that People might talk.
Zhong, there is nothing wrong with you,

But it is the Gossip of others I fear.
That could be truly Awful!

Possibly a slightly satirical piece. The protagonist may be a suitor, but again we have no clear evidence of this. Her concern for public and personal opinion is a nice human touch.

Antique Bell (detail)   Mount Emei

I Followed Him

遵大路兮，掺执子之祛兮，无我恶兮，不寁故也！
遵大路兮，掺执子之手兮，无我魗兮，不寁好也！

Zūn dàlù xī, càn zhí zǐ zhī qū xī, wú wǒ è xī, bù zǎn gù yě!
Zūn dàlù xī, càn zhí zǐ zhī shǒu xī, wú wǒ chǒu xī, bù zǎn hǎo yě!

I FOLLOWED HIM down the Roadway,
I grasped at him by the Sleeve.
I cried, 'Do not hate me!
Not so quick an old Friend to leave.'

I followed him down the Roadway,
I grasped his Hand in mine.
I cried, 'Do not turn from me!
Not so quick our Love to resign.'

A brief song, redolent with meaning. Niu Yunzhen during the Qing Dynasty commented 'her grievance is exquisitely touching; her mood follows a thousand twists and turns'. Powerful.

No-One Here

山有扶苏，隰有荷华。不见子都，乃见狂且。
山有乔松，隰有游龙，不见子充，乃见狡童！

Shān yǒu fú sū, xí yǒu hé huá. Bùjiàn zi dōu, nǎi jiàn kuáng qiě.
Shān yǒu qiáo sōng, xí yǒu yóu long. Bùjiàn zi chōng, nǎi jiàn jiǎo tóng!

ON THE HILL grows the Mulberry tree,
By the Marsh, the Water-lily.
There is no fair Boy I see here,
Just one gormless and silly!

On the Hill stands the lofty Pine,
By the Marsh, the wandering Vetch.
There is no-one Handsome I see here -
Just some juvenile Wretch!

The woman, possibly a courtesan (or prostitute) is teasing her man. Needless to say, sexual morality in early China was multi-layered, as in the West. Or maybe the woman is making fun of her lover, making him the butt of her jokes. The text is fairly opaque.

You Crazy, Crazy Boy

彼狡童兮，不与我言兮。维子之故，使我不能餐兮。
彼狡童兮，不与我食兮。维子之故，使我不能息兮。

Bǐ jiǎo tóng xī, bù yǔ wǒ yán xī.
Wéi zǐ zhī gù, shǐ wǒ bùnéng cān xī.
Bǐ jiǎo tóng xī, bù yǔ wǒ shí xī.
Wéi zǐ zhī gù, shǐ wǒ bùnéng xī xī.

YOU CRAZY, CRAZY BOY!
Do not talk to me no more when We meet!
Because of you my Lad, I cannot eat!

You crazy, crazy Boy!
You'll never again be my Guest!
Because of you my Lad, I can never rest!

   Another short song, in two stanzas. The women has either been abandoned, or betrayed by her young beau. Is she sincere, or merely teasing? The great Song Confucian Zhuxi believed, as in the last poem, that the singer is a prostitute. Chen Jikui during the Qing Dynasty commented: "If she's angry, it's regretful, if she's jesting, it rings true. A most emotional piece." Well said!

A Challenge

子惠思我，褰裳涉溱。子不我思…
岂无他人？狂童之狂也且！
子惠思我，褰裳涉洧。子不我思…
岂无他士？狂童之狂也且！

Zi huì sī wǒ, qiān shang shè qín. Zi bù wǒ sī…
Qǐ wú tārén? Kuáng tóng zhī kuáng yě qiě!
Zi huì sī wǒ, qiān shang shè wěi. Zi bù wǒ sī…
Qǐ wú tā shì? Kuáng tóng zhī kuáng yě qiě!

IF, MY BOY, your Thoughts were kind,
I'd lift my Skirt and wade the Qin.
But if You have someone else in Mind…
   So is there anybody, then?
   You crazy, foolish Boy!

If, my Boy, your Thoughts were kind,
I'd lift my Skirt and wade the Wei.
But if You have someone else in Mind…
   So is there anybody, eh?
   You crazy, foolish Boy!

The woman is angry and accusatory, and she stays away from her man. If he were 'kind', and treated her properly…well, it would be different. She suspects he is seeing someone else. The river Wei flowed through her homeland, eventually merging with the Qin.

Misery Me

子之丰兮，俟我乎巷兮，悔予不送兮。
子之昌兮，俟我乎堂兮，悔予不将兮。
衣锦褧衣，裳锦褧裳。叔兮伯兮，驾予与行!
裳锦褧裳，衣锦褧衣。叔兮伯兮，驾予与归!

Zǐ zhī fēng xī, qí wǒ hū xiàng xī, huǐ yú bù sòng xī.
Zǐ zhī chāng xī, qí wǒ hū táng xī, huǐ yú bù jiāng xī.
Yī jǐn jiǒng yī, shang jǐn jiǒng shang. Shū xī bó xī, jià yǔ yǔ xíng!
Shang jǐn jiǒng shang, yī jǐn jiǒng yī. Shū xī bó xī, jià yǔ yǔ guī!

OH, WHAT an upright, handsome Man!
Waiting for me in the Lane.
I am sad I did not go with him,
That he had to wait in Vain!

Oh, what a strapping, handsome Man!
Waiting for me in the Hall.
I am sad I did not go with him,
But it was not for me at all!

My simple, plain Shawl I'll throw.
Over my embroidered Skirt and Robe.
Now good Sir, good Sir,
Have your Horse ready for me on the Road!

Over my embroidered Robe and Skirt
My simple, plain Shawl I'll throw.
Now good Sir, good Sir,
Have your Horse ready, let us go!

An awkward scene. The girl, uncertain, is then jilted by her man - and then immediately finds another! and cannot wait.

Beyond The Eastern Gate

东门之墠,茹藘在阪。其室则迩,其人甚远。
东门之栗,有践家室。岂不尔思?子不我即!

*Dōng mén zhī shàn, rú lǘ zài bǎn. Qí shì zé ěr, qí rén shén yuǎn.
Dōng mén zhī lì, yǒu jiàn jiā shì. Qǐ bù ěr sī? Zǐ bù wǒ jí!*

THERE BEYOND the Eastern Gate
Where the Flat Lands lie all round.
Where the Madder grows about the Mound.
  His Home quite close can be found,
  But He has become distant to me.

There beyond the Eastern Gate
Where the Chestnut trees still grow.
Where there are those Houses, all in a Row.
  You think I have forgotten you?
  But it is You who never notice me!

The lady here is attached to the place where they last met. What tangles men and woman make for themselves - no wonder Confucius said the Airs of Zheng State (Mao 75-95) made him feel uncomfortable!

Home Again

风雨凄凄，鸡鸣喈喈！
既见君子，云胡不夷！
风雨潇潇，鸡鸣胶胶！
既见君子，云胡不瘳！
风雨如晦，鸡鸣不已！
既见君子，云胡不喜！

Fēngyǔ qī qī, jī míng jiē jiē!
Jì jiàn jūnzǐ, yún hú bù yí.
Fēngyǔ xiāoxiāo, jī míng jiāo jiāo!
Jì jiàn jūnzǐ, yún hú bù chōu!
Fēngyǔ rú huì, jī míng bùyǐ!
Jì jiàn jūnzǐ, yún hú bù xǐ!

HERE COMES the wind,
Here comes the rain!
The cocks crow cock-a-doo!
But my good man I have found again,
So I am contented too!

Wild is the wind,
Wild is the rain!
The cocks crow cock-a-dee!
But my good man I have found again,
And my life has come back to me!

Dark now is the wind
And dark the rain,
The cocks unceasingly call!
But my good man I have found again,
Great joy and happiness to all!

The verses show the happy lot of the wife, now that her husband is home. Bird-calls were often seen as omens in ancient China. A sentiment simple and direct.

Left Just us Few

扬之水，不流束楚。终鲜兄弟，维予与女。
无信人之言，人实诳女。
扬之水，不流束薪。终鲜兄弟，维予二人。
无信人之言，人实不信。

Yáng zhī shuǐ, bù liú shù chǔ. Zhōng xiān xiōngdì, wéi yǔ yǔ nǚ.
Wú xìnrén zhī yán, rén shí kuáng nǚ.
Yáng zhī shuǐ, bù liú shù xīn. Zhōng xiān xiōngdì, wéi yǔ èr rén.
Wú xìnrén zhī yán, rén shí bùxìn.

THAT WINDING Current fails to float
The Bundle of Thorns away.
In Truth there are but Few of us left,
Only You and I, out of the Rest.
   Do not believe the Words of Others,
   They will lead you far Astray!

That winding Current fails to float
The Bundle of Branches away.
In truth there are just left us Few,
Perhaps only us remaining Two.
   Do not believe the Words of Others.
   The Stories they tell are Untrue!

The context of their relationship is unclear. However the warning is stark - we need to stick together.

Creeping Plants Grow Wild

野有蔓草，零露漙兮。
有美一人，清扬婉兮！
邂逅相遇，适我愿兮！
野有蔓草，零露瀼瀼。
有美一人，婉如清扬！

Yě yǒu màncǎo, líng lù tuán xī.
Yǒu měi yì rén, qīng yáng wǎn xī.
Xièhòu xiāngyù, shì wǒ yuàn xī.
Yě yǒu màncǎo, líng lù ráng ráng.
Yǒu měi yì rén, wǎn rú qīng yáng.
Xièhòu xiāngyù, yǔ zi xié zāng.

WHERE CREEPING PLANTS grow wild,
And heavy Dews oft' fall,
I met alone a handsome Man.
Bright-eyed and kind, the Best of all!
  Chance brought me to another's Side,
  And all my Wishes gratified!

Where creeping Plants grow wild,
And the heavy Dews still fall,
I met alone a handsome Man.
Good-looking, Eyes and Forehead all.
  Chance led me to meet Him there,
  Such Joy and Happiness to share!

Yet another simple song about the auspicious meeting of woman and man. Poetic, romantic and charming.

Spring Love-making

溱与洧，方涣涣兮。士与女，方秉蕑兮。
女曰观乎？士曰既且！
且往观乎，洧之外，洵訏且乐。
维士与女，伊其相谑，赠之以勺药。
溱与洧，浏其清矣。士与女，殷其盈矣。
女曰观乎？士曰既且！
且往观乎，洧之外，洵訏且乐。
维士与女，伊其将谑，赠之以勺药。

Qín yǔ wěi, fānghuànhuàn xī. Shì yǔ nǚ, fāngbǐngjiān xī.
Nǚ yuē guān hū? Shì yuē jì qiě!
Qiě wǎng guān hū, wěi zhī wài, xún xū qiě lè.
Wéi shì yǔ nǚ, yī qí xiāng xuè, zèng zhī yǐ sháo yào.
Qín yǔ wěi, liú qí qīng yǐ. Shì yǔ nǚ, yīnqíyíng yǐ.
Nǚ yuē guān hū? Shì yuē jì qiě!
Qiě wǎng guān hū, wěi zhī wài, xún xū qiě lè.
Wéi shì yǔ nǚ, yī qí jiāng xuè, zèng zhī yǐ sháo yào.

WHEN THE RIVER ZHEN and River Wei
Flood out and expand,
Then off go the Youngsters, Valerian in Hand.
  'Are you ready?' ask the Girls.
  'We're up for it!', They reply.
And being up for it, off They go,
Beyond the Wei, to a Place they know.
And there They are happy,
Joined together as Boy and Girl.
There they joke and tease each other,
And each gives the other a Peony, as Token.

As the River Zhen and River Wei
Flood deep and clear,
Boys and Girls in Crowds appear.
  'Are you ready?' ask the Girls.
  'We're up for it!', They reply.
And being ready, off They go,
Beyond the Wei, to a Place they know.
And there They are happy,
Joined together as Boy and Girl.
There they joke and tease each other,
And Each gives the other a Peony, as Token.

One of the most notorious songs in the collection. A flirtatious tone and innuendo are obvious. Events such as these were rumoured to happen during the Spring Festival. The rivers in flood suggest physical passion. The line structure is strangely uneven, but a conversational tone is clear, which perhaps is the point. Broadly speaking this is a song about innocent love. Carrying a valerian flower and the gift of the peony confirm this. The setting is in nature.

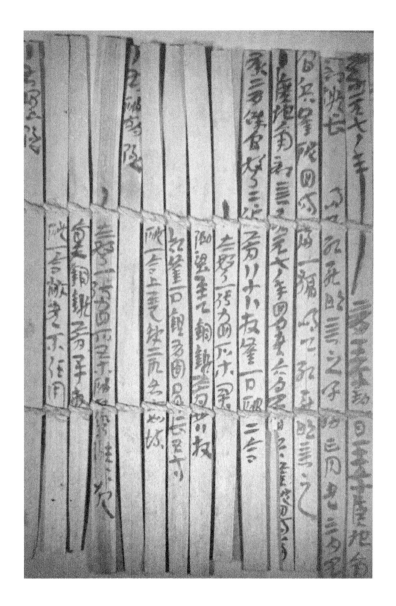

Bamboo Strips – As used before books

The Cock has Crowed

鸡既鸣矣，朝既盈矣。
匪鸡则鸣，苍蝇之声。
东方明矣，朝既昌矣。
匪东方则明，月出之光。
虫飞薨薨，甘与子同梦。
会且归矣，无庶予子憎。

Jī jì míng yǐ, cháo jì yíng yǐ.
Fěi jī zé míng, cāngyíng zhī shēng.
Dōngfāng míng yǐ, cháo jì chāng yǐ.
Fěi dōngfāng zé míng, yuè chū zhī guāng.
Chóng fēi hōng hōng, gān yǔ zǐ tóng mèng.
Huì qiě guī yǐ, wú shù yǔ zi zēng.

'ALREADY the Cock has crowed!
And a Crowd at the Court will be found!'
 'Nay, that was no crowing Cock,
But the Blue-flies buzzing around.'

'The Daylight is in the East!
And it is bright at the Court, so soon!'
 'Nay, that is no Daylight,
Just the Light of the rising Moon.'

'Ah, with the Hum of the Insects here,
T'were sweet to lie dreaming with Thee.
But the Folks there might leave in a While,
And think the Worst of You and Me.'

This song is in dialogue. The woman and man each have two lines in the first two stanzas. In the last, the woman shows her anxieties about 'what the people might think'.

At the Gate He Awaits Me Now

俟我于著乎而，充耳以素乎而，尚之以琼华乎而。
俟我于庭乎而，充耳以青乎而，尚之以琼莹乎而。
俟我于堂乎而，充耳以黄乎而，尚之以琼英乎而。

Qí wǒ yúzhe hū ér, chōng ěr yǐ sù hū ér,
shàngzhī yǐ qióng huá hū ér.
Qí wǒ yú tíng hū ér, chōng ěr yǐ qīng hū ér,
shàngzhī yǐ qióng yíng hū ér.
Qí wǒ yú táng hū ér, chōng ěr yǐ huáng hū ér,
shàngzhī yǐ qióng yīng hū ér.

AT THE GATE HE AWAITS me now,
Quite screened from Sight,
While the Tassels at his Ears are of
The most brilliant white!
And adorned with Gems, gleaming bright!

Now he waits at the Court,
Just past the Screen,
And the Tassels at his Ears are of
The darkest green!
And the Stones have a Lustre seldom seen!

In the Hall at last He awaits,
Just for me, now more bold!
And the Tassels at his Ears are of
The most brilliant gold!
And the Jewels, just fabulous to behold!

A man is proceeding to be wed...the bride's is calm but uneasy, expectant. The exclamatory binome 'hu er' (乎而) repeats nine times, adding a drama all of its own.

Surely Not Him

彼汾沮洳，言采其莫。彼其之子，美无度。
美无度，殊异乎公路。
彼汾一方，言采其桑。彼其之子，美如英。
美如英，殊异乎公行。
彼汾一曲，言采其藚。彼其之子，美如玉。
美如玉，殊异乎公族。

Bǐ fén jù rù, yán cǎi qí mò. Bǐ qí zhīzǐ, měi wúdù.
Měi wúdù, shū yìhū gōnglù.
Bǐ fén yīfāng, yán cǎi qí sāng. Bǐ qí zhīzǐ, měi rú yīng.
Měi rú yīng, shū yìhū gōng xíng.
Bǐ fén yī qū, yán cǎi qí xù. Bǐ qí zhīzǐ, měi rú yù.
Měi rú yù, shū yìhū gōng zú.

I WENT TO THE MARSHES after the River Fan,
To work with the Sorrel Gatherers then.
And soon I saw my nice young Man,
   Such a Beauty beyond compare!
   Such a Beauty beyond compare!
Surely not the 'Warden' picking there!

I went to the Fields beside the River Fan,
To work with the Mulberry Pickers then.
And soon I saw my nice young Man,
   As any Flower fair!
   As any Flower fair!
Surely not the 'Marshal' picking there!

I went to the Marshes beyond the River Fan,
To gather the Oxlip, root and stem.
And soon I saw my nice young Man,
   Bright as any polished Gem!
   Bright as any polished Gem!
Surely not the 'Recorder' picking there!

A young girl walks to work, picking in the fields. She sees her young beau - and fantasizes him as a junior officer of rank. The contrast between the warmth of her heart and the formal titles is touching.

What Might Tonight Bring

绸缪束薪，三星在天。今夕何夕，见此良人？
子兮子兮，如此良人何？
绸缪束刍，三星在隅。今夕何夕，见此邂逅？
子兮子兮，如此邂逅何？
绸缪束楚，三星在户。今夕何夕，见此粲者？
子兮子兮，如此粲者何？

Chóumóu shù xīn, sānxīng zài tiān.
Jīnxī hé xī, jiàn cǐ liáng rén? Zi xī zi xī, rúcǐ liáng rén hé?
Chóumóu shù chú, sānxīng zài yú.
Jīnxī hé xī, jiàn cǐ xièhòu? Zi xī zi xī, rúcǐ xièhòu hé?
Chóumóu shù chǔ, sānxīng zài hù.
Jīnxī hé xī, jiàn cǐ càn zhě? Zi xī zi xī, rúcǐ càn zhě hé?

ALL AROUND THE TWIGS are to be bound,
The Three Stars in the Sky now shine.
   Tonight, what might Tonight bring?
Now I will see this good Man mine!
   Oh me! Oh my!
That a Man like him could come by here!

All around the Grass is to be bound,
The Three Stars in the Sky now clear.
   Tonight, what might Tonight bring!
Meeting him this night, unexpectedly here!
   Oh my! Oh me!
That We should meet again so suddenly!

All around the Thorns are to be bound,
The Three Stars in the Sky at my Door.
   Tonight, what might Tonight bring!
That I am to see the One I adore!
   Oh my! Oh me!
However came such a Man to me!

   'A girl is carrying out her chores waiting for her lover. As the time creeps closer so the stars seem to be brighter. Binding the twigs and grasses suggests their growing relationship.

All Alone

葛生蒙楚，蔹蔓于野！
予美亡此，谁与？独处？
葛生蒙棘，蔹蔓于域！
予美亡此，谁与？独息！
角枕粲兮，锦衾烂兮。
予美亡此，谁与？独旦？
夏之日，冬之夜。百岁之后，归于其居。
冬之夜，夏之日。百岁之后，归于其室。

Géshēng méng chǔ, liǎn màn yú yě!
Yǔ měi wáng cǐ, shéi yǔ? Dúchǔ?
Géshēng méng jí, liǎn màn yú yù!
Yǔ měi wáng cǐ, shéi yǔ? Dú xī!
Jiǎo zhěn càn xī, jǐn qīn làn xī.
Yǔ měi wáng cǐ, shéi yǔ? Dú dàn?
Xià zhī rì, dōng zhī yè. Bǎi suì zhīhòu, guīyú qí jū.
Dōng zhī yè, xià zhī rì. Bǎi suì zhīhòu, guīyú qí shì.

THE BEANS CREEP UP to choke that Bush!
And in the Wasteland, Weeds have spread.
Now my loved One's left me alone.
I'm all by Myself, so why go to Bed?

The Beans creep on to choke that Thorn!
While cross the Graves, a Bramble grows.
Now my loved One has deserted me here,
To be a Loner. It's not what I chose!

My Horn Pillow is so beautiful!
My figured Bedspread looks so gay!
And my loved One has left me here,
All by Myself - waiting for the Day.

Through Summer Days and Winter Nights,
One hundred Years, I'll stay at Home....
Through Winter Nights and Summer Days,
Hundred Years hence, I'll return alone!

The woman (or possibly man) has been abandoned. It is not what she would have chosen. Gradually she returns to herself - and by the turn of the year begins to come to terms with being single.

My Thoughts are All with My Man

小戎俴收，五楘梁辀。游环胁驱，阴靷鋈续。
文茵畅毂，驾我骐馵。
言念君子，温其如玉。在其板屋，乱我心曲。
四牡孔阜，六辔在手。骐骝是中，騧骊是骖。
龙盾之合，鋈以觼軜。
言念君子，温其在邑。方何为期？胡然我念之。
俴驷孔群，厹矛鋈錞。蒙伐有苑，虎韔镂膺。
交韔二弓，竹闭绲縢。
言念君子，载寝载兴。厌厌良人，秩秩德音。

Xiǎo róng jiàn shōu, wǔ mù liáng zhōu. Yóu huán xié qū,
yīn yǐn wù xù. Wén yīn chàng gǔ, jià wǒ qí zhù.
Yán niàn jūnzǐ, wēnqírú yù. Zài qí bǎnwū, luàn wǒ xīnqū.
Sì mǔ kǒng fù, liù pèi zài shǒu. Qí liú shì zhōng, guā lí shì
cān. Lóng dùn zhī hé, wù yǐ jué nà.
Yán niàn jūnzǐ, wēn qí zài yì. Fāng hé wéiqí?
Hú rán wǒ niàn zhī.
Jiàn sì kǒng qún, róu máo wù chún. Méng fá yǒu yuàn,
hǔ chàng lòu yīng. Jiāo chàng èr gōng, zhú bì gǔn téng.
Yán niàn jūnzǐ, zài qǐn zài xìng.
Yàn yàn liáng rén, zhì zhì dé yīn.

HIS TIDY CARRIAGE with its glistening Plate,
With its Pole and tight Ribbon-bindings,
   Sliding Rings and Shoulder-braces,
Silver Fastenings at the Cross-bar,
A tiger-skin Mat, the running Hubs,
   And my Piebald at the Traces!

But my Thoughts are all with my Man,
   My Man so precious, so kind.
When will he return to our Home?
   He puts this Worry into my Mind!

His Team of four young Colts, tugging
With several tight Reins to control them,
   The Piebald and Bay pulling within,
The dappled Grey beside them,
The Dragon-shields along the Sides,
   And silver-gilt Buckles to fix them.

But my Thoughts are all with my Man,
   He gets on so well with the Crowd!
When, O when will his Time be ended?
   Oh, my Thoughts! they cry out loud!

His fine four Chargers, pulling well,
The trident Spears with metalled Ends,
   His shiny feather-figured Shield,
And tiger-skin Bow-case, mounted,
With both Bows bound inside the Case,
   And to the Frame both tied and sealed.

But my Thoughts are all with my Man,
   When I get up and when I lie down.
Worthy Fellow, may he come Home safe,
   And his Name find wide renown.

A lengthy description of the magnificence of a war-carriage and team. Yet the grandeur of the carriage pales against the anxious thoughts of the wife and her evident concern is mingled with pride.

Where Reed and Rush

蒹葭苍苍，白露为霜。所谓伊人，在水一方。
溯洄从之，道阻且长。溯游从之，宛在水中央！
蒹葭萋萋，白露未晞。所谓伊人，在水之湄。
溯洄从之，道阻且跻。溯游从之，宛在水中坻！
蒹葭采采，白露未已。所谓伊人，在水之涘。
溯洄从之，道阻且右。溯游从之，宛在水中沚！

Jiānjiā cāngcāng, báilù wèi shuāng. Suǒwèi yīrén, zài shuǐ yīfāng.
Sù huí cóng zhī, dào zǔ qiě zhǎng. Sù yóu cóng zhī, wǎn zài shuǐ zhōngyāng!
Jiānjiā qī qī, báilù wèi xī. Suǒwèi yīrén, zài shuǐ zhī méi.
Sù huí cóng zhī, dào zǔ qiě jī. Sù yóu cóng zhī, wǎn zài shuǐ zhōng chí!
Jiānjiā cǎi cǎi, báilù wèi yǐ. Suǒwèi yīrén, zài shuǐ zhī sì.
Sù huí cóng zhī, dào zǔ qiě yòu. Sù yóu cóng zhī, wǎn zài s huǐ zhōng zhǐ!

WHERE REED and rush grow rich and green,
And the white Dew to Hoar-frost changes,
The fellow they speak of as 'that Man ',
Goes 'bout on the river Ranges.
Upstream I went to find him,
A long and tiresome Way.
Downstream I went,
But all the Time Mid-stream he lay!

Where Reed and Rush grow deep and tall,
And the white Dew as yet's undried,
The fellow they speak of as 'that Man ',
I thought he was by the Riverside.
Upstream I went to find him,
The Path bouldered and steep.
Downstream I went to the Islet,
But he was Mid-stream asleep!

Where Reed and Rush grow tall and thick,
And the white Dew lingers dank,
The fellow they speak of as 'that Man ',
I thought he was on the river's Bank.
Upstream I went to find him,
In the rough on the other Side.

Downs I went but on a rocky Crop
Mid-stream, he chose to hide!

A girl cannot find her fellow. She searches up and down the river and finally finds him midstream asleep, probably on an islet. A humorous piece.

My Worried Heart

鴥彼晨风，郁彼北林。未见君子，
忧心钦钦。如何如何，忘我实多！
山有苞栎，隰有六驳。未见君子，
忧心靡乐。如何如何，忘我实多！
山有苞棣，隰有树檖。未见君子，
忧心如醉。如何如何，忘我实多！

Yù bǐ chén fēng, yù bǐ běilín. Wèi jiàn jūnzǐ,
yōuxīn qīn qīn. Rúhé rúhé, wàngwǒ shí duō!
Shān yǒu bāo lì, xí yǒu liù bó. Wèi jiàn jūnzǐ,
yōuxīn mí lè. Rúhé rúhé, wàngwǒ shí duō!
Shān yǒu bāo dì, xí yǒu shù suì. Wèi jiàn jūnzǐ,
yōuxīn rú zuì. Rúhé rúhé, wàngwǒ shí duō!

SWIFTLY SPEEDS the Sparrow-hawk,
North to where the dark Woods grow.
He's still away, my worried Heart!
He went so long ago.
How can it be, He chooses to forget!

The Oaks grow densely on the Hill
And Elms, six of them, in the Mead.
But He's still away, my worried Heart!
   A dull Life I lead.
How can it be, He chooses to forget!

On the Hill grow the Cherry-plums,
And by the Mead, the wild Pears.
And He's still away, my worried Heart!
   I am sunk amidst my cares.
How can it be, He chooses to forget!

Again, one of many songs about separation. She is acutely worried about his absence. Is he at war, or on business? It is not clear. She also expresses a pang of righteous anger.

What a Night!

东门之杨，其叶牂牂。昏以为期，明星煌煌。
东门之杨，其叶肺肺。昏以为期，明星晢晢。

Dōng mén zhī yáng, qí yè zāng zāng.
Hūn yǐwéi qī, míngxīng huánghuáng.
Dōng mén zhī yáng, qí yè fèi fèi.
Hūn yǐwéi qī, míngxīng zhé zhé.

LOOK AT the Willows at Eastern Gate,
Their Leaves just beginning to show green.
At Twilight I first met up with you -
Now the Morning Star's burns,
   What a Night it's been!

Look at the Willows at the Eastern Gate,
Their Leaves starting to show a soft Sheen.
At Twilight I went to meet with you -
Now the Morning Star's bright,
   What a Night it's been!

A delicately pencilled-in picture of some kind of all-night tryst. It is what is not said here that is so important. Was she/he waiting for a secret assignment? political intrigue? or romance? The jury is out, so make your own judgement!

134

At the Margin of the Moor

彼泽之陂，有蒲与荷。有美一人，伤如之何？
　　寤寐无为，涕泗滂沱。
彼泽之陂，有蒲与蕳。有美一人，硕大且卷。
　　寤寐无为，中心悁悁。
彼泽之陂，有蒲菡萏。有美一人，硕大且俨。
　　寤寐无为，辗转伏枕。

*Bǐ zé zhī bēi, yǒu pú yǔ hé. Yǒu měi yì rén, shāng rú zhī hé?
Wù mèi wúwéi, tì sì pāngtuó.
Bǐ zé zhī bēi, yǒu pú yǔ jiān. Yǒu měi yì rén, shuòdà qiě juǎn.
Wù mèi wúwéi, zhōngxīn yuān yuān.
Bǐ zé zhī bēi, yǒu pú hàn dàn. Yǒu měi yì rén, shuòdà qiě yǎn. Wù mèi wúwéi, niǎnzhuǎn fú zhěn.*

AT THE MARGIN OF THE MOOR,
Water-lilies and Rushes grow.
And there lives the noblest of Men.
But I am broken, and nothing know.
   Waking , sleeping, I do nothing,
   Nothing, but snivelling Tears.

At the Margin of the Moor,
Rushes grow and sweet Valerian.
Tall, broad and handsome,
He was surely the noblest of Men.
   Waking , sleeping, I do nothing,
   My Heart just so full of Grief!

At the Margin of the Moor,
Grow the Rushes and the Lotus.
There lived the noblest of all Men.
Tall, imposing, and whom All notice!
   Waking , sleeping, I do nothing.
   But turn over, bury my Face in the Pillow.

A painfully honest song about a break-up. We are not allowed any context - the lines simply focus on the woman's tears and relentless grief.

Are You Still Loitering

羔裘逍遥，狐裘以朝。岂不尔思！劳心忉忉。
羔裘翱翔，狐裘在堂。岂不尔思！我心忧伤。
羔裘如膏，日出有曜。岂不尔思！中心是悼！

Gāo qiú xiāoyáo, hú qiúyǐcháo.
Qǐ bù ěr sī? Láoxīn dāo dāo.
Gāo qiú áoxiáng, hú qiúzàitáng.
Qǐ bù ěr sī? Wǒ xīn yōushāng.
Gāo qiú rú gāo, rì chū yǒu yào.
Qǐ bù ěr sī? Zhōngxīn shì dào!

ARE YOU IN your Lambskin still loitering
And in your Fox-fur, sitting at Court?
You say I should not be anxious!
But my are of the worrying Sort.

Still in your Lambskin loitering.
And in your Fox-fur, going to the Hall?
You say I should not be anxious!
But in Pain and Sadness, I notice All.

Now in your Lambskin, it shines with Grease.
It still glistens like the morning Sun!
You say I should not be anxious!
But in my Heart I am quite undone!

The truth is out - he cares more about appearances, than his courtly office. Probably the complaint of a dutiful wife.

The Fragility of Life

蜉蝣之羽，衣裳楚楚。
心之忧矣，於我归处。
蜉蝣之翼，采采衣服。
心之忧矣，於我归息。
蜉蝣掘阅，麻衣如雪。
心之忧矣，於我归说。

Fúyóu zhī yǔ, yīshang chǔchǔ.
Xīn zhī yōu yǐ, yú wǒ guī chù.
Fúyóu zhī yì, cǎi cǎi yīfú.
Xīn zhī yōu yǐ, yú wǒ guī xī.
Fúyóu jué yuè, máyī rú xuě.
Xīn zhī yōu yǐ, yú wǒ guī shuō.

O, the Mayflies' Wings!
And the way They're dressed!
Yet my Heart is now failing –
So homeward is best.

O, the Mayflies' Wings!
What have They got on?
Yet my Heart is now failing –
And I'll have to be gone.

See the Chrysalis burst!
And its Insides like Snow!
Yet my Heart is now failing –
So homeward I'll go.

The mayfly can live but a moment, which sparks the thought that life is so extremely fragile, and fleeting. Thus she speaks of returning home. As I stress in the Introduction, many of verses in the Book of Songs talk of home.

Biography

Richard Bertschinger has had a lifetime interest in old China. His philosophy degree led him to explore Chinese texts in translation, but this quickly led to study with Giafu Feng (1919-1986), Bill Tara, Ischa Bloomberg, Jack Worsley d.2003, among others, and at Chengdu Medical College, Sichuan (1986). He learnt to read and, more importantly, decipher the ancient script. His translations include: *The Golden Needle* 1991, *The Secret of Everlasting Life* 1994, *The Great Intent* 2013, *Some Jottings on Contentment* 2019, *Fifty Zen Koans 2022* and *Hot-Air Ballooning with the Han Chine*se 2023. He is also working on a Shamanic Yijing. He lives in Somerset UK, in addition to practicing Qigong and Acupuncture.

Printed in Great Britain
by Amazon